# Living Green at Home

## Molly Aloian

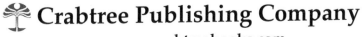
Crabtree Publishing Company

www.crabtreebooks.com

**Author**
Molly Aloian

**Publishing plan research and development**
Reagan Miller

**Editor**
Rachel Eagen

**Proofreader and indexer**
Wendy Scavuzzo

**Design**
Samara Parent

**Photo research**
Samara Parent

**Production coordinator
and prepress technician**
Samara Parent

**Print coordinator**
Margaret Amy Salter

**Photographs**
Dreamstime: page 16
Thinkstock: cover, title page, pages 8, 13, 14, 19 (top), 21
All other images by Shutterstock

**Library and Archives Canada Cataloguing in Publication**

Aloian, Molly, author
    Living green at home / Molly Aloian.

(The green scene)
Includes index.
Issued in print and electronic formats.
ISBN 978-0-7787-0274-0 (bound).--ISBN 978-0-7787-0285-6
(pbk.).--ISBN 978-1-4271-1270-5 (pdf).--ISBN 978-1-4271-9439-8
(html)

        1. Sustainable living--Juvenile literature.  I. Title.

GE195.5.A56 2013          j333.72          C2013-905211-9
                                           C2013-905212-7

**Library of Congress Cataloging-in-Publication Data**

Aloian, Molly.
  Living green at home / Molly Aloian.
      pages cm. --  (The green scene)
  Includes index.
  ISBN 978-0-7787-0274-0 (reinforced library binding) -- ISBN 978-0-7787-
0285-6 (pbk.) -- ISBN 978-1-4271-1270-5 (electronic pdf) -- ISBN 978-1-4271-
9439-8 (electronic html)
  1.  Environmentalism--Juvenile literature. 2.  Sustainable living--Juvenile
literature.  I. Title.

  GE195.5.A47 2014
  640.28'6--dc23
                                                   2013030086

# Crabtree Publishing Company

www.crabtreebooks.com          1-800-387-7650

Printed in the U.S.A./092014/CG20140808

**Published in Canada**
**Crabtree Publishing**
616 Welland Ave.
St. Catharines, Ontario
L2M 5V6

**Published in the United States**
**Crabtree Publishing**
PMB 59051
350 Fifth Avenue, 59th Floor
New York, New York 10118

**Published in the United Kingdom**
**Crabtree Publishing**
Maritime House
Basin Road North, Hove
BN41 1WR

**Published in Australia**
**Crabtree Publishing**
3 Charles Street
Coburg North
VIC 3058

# Contents

# Living green

Living green means doing things to lessen our **impact** on Earth. To lessen our impact, we must make small changes in our lives. We must buy less and throw away less garbage. We must use less energy and try to **conserve** all of Earth's **natural resources**. We have to cause less **pollution** and use environmentally-friendly products.

Cars and factories burn tons of *fossil fuels* every day. Fumes from the burning fuel make the air, land, and water dirty and polluted.

4

## Take Action!

Water is an important natural resource. Clean, fresh drinking water is very precious and we need to make sure we do not waste it. How can you stop wasting water?

# Create a green kitchen

There are many ways to live green at home. The kitchen is a great place to start. Ask your parents to buy loose vegetables and fruit without any packaging. **Reuse** plastic containers, aluminum foil, plastic wrap, and other food packaging. The less you throw away, the less garbage ends up in **landfills**.

*Living green at home means eating fresh fruits and vegetables and trying to avoid packaged foods.*

# Get unplugged

Unplug the toaster, blender, and other small kitchen appliances when you are not using them. Doing so burns fewer fossil fuels and saves energy.

*Before using the dishwasher, make sure it is completely full of dirty dishes to save energy and water.*

# A green living room

One of the easiest ways to live green at home is to change a few light bulbs in your living room, family room, or den. Try to use energy-efficient light bulbs instead of regular light bulbs. They use less energy, last longer, and provide the same amount of light.

*Energy-efficient light bulbs use up to 80% less energy than regular light bulbs.*

8

## Turn it off

Be sure to turn off lights, TVs, DVD players, and video game consoles when you are not using them. Save energy and money by not leaving computers and other electronics on standby, or in "sleep mode."

*Instead of watching TV every evening, play a board game with your family, or play outside with friends. You will save energy and have fun.*

# A better bedroom

Ask an adult to help you fix and repaint old or broken furniture and fix up old toys. You can also donate your gently-used things to a second-hand store so that someone else can use them. This is much more Earth-friendly than throwing them away!

Shopping at second-hand stores is fun! You never know what treasures you may find.

## Make the most of it

Doing so keeps garbage out of landfills and makes the most of the time, money, materials, and energy used to make the items. This is part of what it means to live green at home.

*Old toys are often easy to fix. Glue, sew, and patch toys instead of throwing them in the garbage.*

# Clean, green closet

Never throw old clothes or shoes into the garbage. There are many ways to reuse them. Add colorful patches, buttons, or other decorations to old clothes to make them feel like new again. Keep old clothes for messy jobs such as painting. Plant flowers in old shoes or boots. Take old clothes and shoes to a second-hand store.

*Save water and money by running the washing machine only when you have a full load.*

12

**Take Action!**

Hang wet clothes on an outdoor clothesline to dry instead of putting them in the dryer. Your clothes will dry faster in the sun and you will save energy.

13

# Green bathroom

There are plenty of ways to be green in the bathroom. Turn off the tap while you brush your teeth. Take a fast shower instead of a bath. Try to flush the toilet less. Ask your parents to buy toilet paper made from **recycled** paper.

*When you brush your teeth, use a cup of water to rinse your mouth and your toothbrush. Never let the tap run.*

## Phosphate-free

Many kinds of soap, shampoo, and other bathroom products contain harmful **phosphates** that are bad for the environment. They wash down the drain and cause pollution. When shopping, read labels and look for bathroom products that are friendly to the environment.

Take Action!

*When you take a shower, turn off the water when you are lathering your hair and body. You will help save hundreds of gallons of water in just one month.*

# Green cleaning

Many household cleaners, such as bleach and oven cleaners, contain **chemicals** that are bad for the environment. They get into waterways and cause pollution. Ask your parents to buy or make their own environmentally-friendly cleaning products. Clean your clothes with environmentally-friendly laundry detergent.

*Harsh chemicals in cleaning products are bad for your health. Try using green products you can make yourself!*

Lemon juice, cooking oil, vinegar, and baking soda are just a few environmentally-friendly cleaning products. Ask your parents to use these for cleaning instead of harmful household cleaners.

Olive Oil

SALT

White Vinegar

Sodium Bicarbonate

# Living green outside

There are many ways to live green outside. The trees, shrubs, and flowers in your backyard provide homes for birds, insects, and other animals. Trees and other plants also help keep the air clean by removing harmful **carbon dioxide** from Earth's atmosphere. Collect rainwater in a barrel and use it to water grass and other plants in your yard.

*Worms help make compost. They eat the rotting food and yard waste and help change it into dark brown soil.*

*Compost bin*

## Making compost

Kitchen and yard waste, including egg shells, fruit and vegetable peels, coffee grounds, grass clippings, and dead leaves, can be recycled and turned into **compost** in an outdoor bin. People use compost to help plants grow.

# Other ways to be green

There are many other ways to be green. If you go to a park for a picnic, do not leave any garbage behind. Recycle and try to think of new ways to reuse everything you can. If you go to the grocery store with your parents, make sure to bring reusable bags instead of plastic bags.

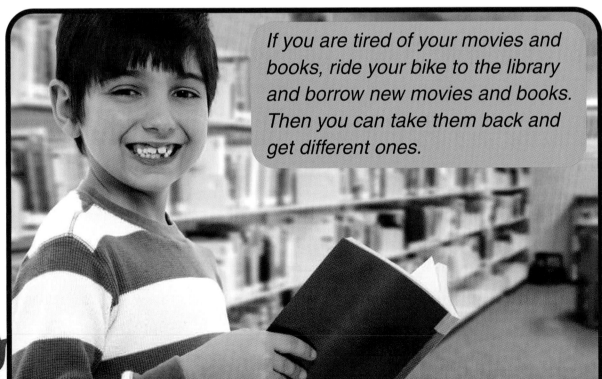

*If you are tired of your movies and books, ride your bike to the library and borrow new movies and books. Then you can take them back and get different ones.*

**YARD SALE**

Instead of throwing away old books and toys, have a garage sale. This is a fun way to earn a little money and get rid of books or toys that you no longer use.

# How green is your home?

Take the quiz below to find out how green your home is. You will find the greenest answers at the bottom of this page.

## Question 1

What do you see inside your refrigerator?

☐ Vegetables and fruit in plastic packaging

☐ Loose vegetables and fruit

☐ Some fruit in packaging, but loose vegetables

## Question 2

What kind of light bulbs does your family use?

☐ No light bulbs

☐ Regular light bulbs

☐ Energy-efficient light bulbs

## Question 3

When you brush your teeth, you:

☐ Let the tap run

☐ Always turn off the tap

☐ Sometimes forget to turn off the tap

**Answers:**
Question 1—
Loose vegetables
and fruit, Question
2—Energy-
efficient light
bulbs, Question
3—Always turn off
the tap

22

# Learning more

## Books

Dunn, Jill. *The ABCs of Going Green*. AuthorMike Ink, 2012.

Gaarder-Juntti, Oona. *What in the World Is a Green Home?*
Super Sandcastle, 2010.

Kalman, Bobbie. *The ABCs of the Environment* (The ABCs of the Natural
World). Crabtree Publishing Company, 2009.

Parenzan Smalley, Carol. *Green Changes You Can Make Around Your Home*.
Mitchell Lane Publishers, 2010.

## Websites

Kids Be Green
http://kidsbegreen.org/

Ten Tips for a Green Home
http://www.treehugger.com/culture/ten-tips-for-a-green-home.html

U.S. Energy Information Administration: Energy Kids
http://www.eia.gov/kids/

U.S. Environmental Protection Agency: Green Homes
http://www.epa.gov/greenhomes/

# Words to know

Note: Some boldfaced words are defined where they appear in the book.

**carbon dioxide** (KAHR-buhn dahy-OK-sahyd) noun  A gas made up of carbon and oxygen that is present in air

**chemicals** (KEM-i-kuhlz) noun  Unnatural things that cause harm to the environment

**compost** (KOM-pohst) noun  A mixture of waste, such as dead leaves or vegetable peels, that has broken down and changed into rich soil for plants

**conserve** (kuhn-SURV) verb  To use carefully or keep safe

**fossil fuels** (FOS-uhl FYOO-uhlz) noun  Fuels such as oil, natural gas, and coal that are used to power cars, make electricity, and heat and cool homes

**impact** (IM-pakt) noun  A strong or forceful effect

**landfills** (LAND-filz) noun  Huge holes in the ground that are filled with garbage and then covered with soil

**natural resources** (NACH-er-uh-l REE-sawrs-ez) noun  Useful materials, such as trees and water, that are found in nature

**phosphates** (FOS-feyts) noun  Salts of phosphoric acid

**pollution** (puh-LOO-shuhn)  noun Chemicals, fumes, waste, or garbage that harm or spoil Earth

**recycled** (ree-SAHY-kuhl-d) verb  Changed or processed to be used again, sometimes in a different way

**reuse** (ree-YOOZ) verb  To use something again

*A noun is a person, place, or thing.*
*An adjective is a word that tells you what something looks like.*
*A verb is an action word that tells you what someone or something does.*

# Index

24